Vocabulary Tests
Level 5

Suitable for ages 11 – 13

Each word study unit contains

- Definition matching
- Cloze sentences

Contents		**Solutions**	
Unit 1	page 2	Unit 1	page 42
Unit 2	page 4	Unit 2	page 42
Unit 3	page 6	Unit 3	page 42
Unit 4	page 8	Unit 4	page 43
Unit 5	page 10	Unit 5	page 43
Unit 6	page 12	Unit 6	page 44
Unit 7	page 14	Unit 7	page 44
Unit 8	page 16	Unit 8	page 44
Unit 9	page 18	Unit 9	page 45
Unit 10	page 20	Unit 10	page 45
Test 1	page 22	Test 1	page 46
Test 2	page 26	Test 2	page 47
Test 3	page 30	Test 3	page 48
Test 4	page 34	Test 4	page 49
Test 5	page 38	Test 5	page 50

Copyright © 2017 Simon Steggels
All rights reserved

No part of this book may be reproduced, stored in a retrieval system, communicated or transmitted in any form or by any means without prior written permission. All inquiries should be made to the publisher.

ISBN 978-0-6480967-9-5

Published by
Advanced Instruction Pty Ltd
www.advancedinstruction.com.au

Unit 1

Definitions—match the words in the bold with their meanings below

auction	**longingly**	**imposing**	**engineered**
forensic	**leotard**	**Victorian**	**value-added**
hedge	**poise**	**forlorn**	**cholesterol**
diabetes	**instinctively**	**retained**	**genetically-modified**

1. calm confidence in a person's way of behaving, or a quality of grace in the way a person holds or moves their body _____

2. having an appearance that looks important or inspires admiration _____

3. a tight piece of clothing that covers the body but not the legs, usually worn by dancers _____

4. in a way that shows that some action has not been thought about, planned, or developed by training _____

5. public sale of goods or property, where people make higher and higher bids until the goods are sold _____

6. belonging to, made in, or living in the time when Queen Victoria was Queen of Great Britain and Ireland _____

7. related to scientific methods of solving crimes, involving examining objects or substances—evidence—at a crime _____

8. an improvement to something that makes it worth more _____

9. in a way that shows a feeling of wanting something very much _____

10. substance containing fat that is found in the body tissue and blood of all animals _____

11. a disease in which the body cannot control the level of sugar in the blood _____

12. designed and built something using scientific principles; skilfully arranged for something to occur _____

13. kept or continued to have something _____

14. alone and unhappy; left alone and not cared for _____

15. a line of bushes planted very close together, especially along the edge of a garden; to protect or limit something _____

16. plant or animal has had some of its genes changed scientifically _____

Unit 1

Word usage—complete the sentences using the words in bold from the previous page

1. The cereal was advertised as _____ as it included enriched vitamins.

2. Vegetable oil is high in polyunsaturates and low in _____.

3. The family is holding an _____ of their house on Thursday.

4. The men who _____ the bridge received acknowledgement in the opening ceremony.

5. After a close semi-final, she _____ her position at the top of the competition leader board.

6. At six feet, seven inches tall, the actor was an _____ figure on stage.

7. My neighbour's privet _____ is overgrown and in need of pruning.

8. I gazed _____ at the box of chocolates, hoping to be offered one.

9. Type 2 _____ is related to poor diet and a lack of exercise.

10. _____ examination revealed a large quantity of poison in the man's stomach.

11. The woman knew _____ that the man at her door was dangerous.

12. Her confidence and _____ show that she is an accomplished dancer.

13. Charles Dickens is one of the best-known _____ novelists.

14. The farmer planted _____ crops that were designed to resist pests.

15. The old man was a _____ figure standing at the bus stop in the rain.

16. I was required to wear a _____ to jazz ballet lessons.

© MR STEGGELS ADVANCED INSTRUCTION PTY LTD

Unit 2

Definitions—match the words in the bold with their meanings below

economy	**shatter**	**godlike**	**surveillance**
considerations	**evidence**	**obsessed**	**ransom**
essence	**pitch**	**missionaries**	**infrared**
uniformly	**cipher**	**sacred**	**spectrometer**

1. a system of writing that prevents others from understanding a secret message _____
2. careful thoughts about a particular subject before making a decision _____
3. the intentional saving of money, time, energy or words; the management of resources of a country, its productivity _____
4. a large amount of money that is demanded in exchange for someone who has been taken prisoner _____
5. a thick, black substance used to waterproof wooden ships; used to describe complete darkness _____
6. unable to stop thinking or worrying about something _____
7. to end or severely damage something _____
8. in a way that is the same; not changing or different; evenly _____
9. the most important part of something, usually the part that gives it its general character _____
10. having overwhelming strength, size or power _____
11. considered to be holy and deserving respect _____
12. the careful watching of a person or place because of a crime or expected activity _____
13. people who are sent to a foreign country to teach their religion to the people who live there _____
14. a piece of equipment used by scientists to separate ions into groups to measure mass and electrical charge _____
15. a type of light that feels warm but cannot be seen _____
16. reasons for believing that something is or is not true _____

Unit 2

Word usage—complete the sentences using the words in bold from the previous page

1. The aeroplane pilot was guided by an _____ optical system that showed images clearly, even at night.

2. Dr Reynolds will prepare the sample to be analysed in the _____.

3. The gang of criminals held the famous racehorse for _____.

4. Is there any scientific _____ that a person's character is reflected in their handwriting?

5. The police keep the house under _____ because of suspected illegal activity.

6. Noisy motorbikes _____ the peace of quiet, respectable neighbourhoods.

7. Repetitive tasks can be done with greater _____ by machines when compared to humans.

8. It was _____ black and I was lost in the forest, alone.

9. There are several important _____ to be made before selling the house.

10. Many _____ relics were uncovered in the tomb by the archeologists.

11. The desks in the hall were arranged _____ for the examination.

12. The _____ of his argument was that education should be available to all people; not just the wealthy.

13. I often wonder why people are so _____ with money that they let it rule their lives.

14. He was one of several _____ sent by his church to work in Alaska.

15. Superheroes are supposed to possess _____ powers.

16. The message that was intercepted from the enemy was written in _____.

© MR STEGGELS ADVANCED INSTRUCTION PTY LTD

Unit 3

Definitions—match the words in the bold with their meanings below

endowment	mainstream	formidable	monochromatic
in lieu	breach	coronation	micron
ensue	taboo	plundered	home in
unadulterated	belittle	piety	wavelength

1. to make a person or an action seem as if he, she or it is not important _____

2. to happen after something else, especially as a result of it _____

3. a ceremony at which a person is made king or queen _____

4. money that is given to a college, hospital, etc. in order to provide it with an income, or the giving of this money _____

5. large and powerful, causing fear and respect _____

6. instead of _____

7. to make an opening in; the act or result of breaking _____

8. strong belief in a religion shown in the way someone lives _____

9. stole goods violently from a place, especially during a war _____

10. using only black, white, and grey, or only one colour _____

11. an action or word that is avoided for religious or social reasons _____

12. unspoiled by the addition of other substances; pure _____

13. the distance between two waves of energy; the length of the radio wave _____

14. considered normal, and having or using ideas and beliefs that are accepted by most people _____

15. to direct onto a target _____

16. one millionth of a metre _____

Unit 3

Word usage—complete the sentences using the words in bold from the previous page

1. After the royal family fled, the palace was _____ by rebels.

2. The cathedral was overflowing with people wanting to see the King's _____.

3. The library has received an _____ of $50,000 to upgrade its services.

4. There is a _____ against wearing a bikini at the beach.

5. He cleaned my garage _____ of payment for the work I did on his car.

6. A cannon ball had made a _____ in their castle walls.

7. At 120kg, the heavyweight champion was a _____ opponent.

8. The park in winter is a depressing _____ brown.

9. We are expecting a scuffle to _____ when we try to handcuff the suspect.

10. Don't _____ other people for not being as skilled at sport as you are.

11. 'Your dog ate your project?' cried my teacher. 'What _____ nonsense!'

12. Acts of _____ and charity are expected of nuns and priests.

13. The scientific equipment was being calibrated to read accurately to one _____.

14. Using a drone, we were able to _____ on the enemy hideout.

15. The law will allow more people with disabilities to enter _____ society.

16. I located the _____ on which the radio station was broadcasting.

© MR STEGGELS ADVANCED INSTRUCTION PTY LTD

Unit 4

Definitions—match the words in the bold with their meanings below

rights	**expulsion**	**putrid**	**embryo**
funded	**barbarous**	**bearings**	**criticism**
halted	**rudimentary**	**seething**	**orchestrated**
social justice	**pseudonym**	**scenario**	**implanted**

1. decaying and smelling very bad _____
2. sense of place; location _____
3. a name that someone uses that is not their real name, especially for writing a book _____
4. brought to an abrupt stop _____
5. the fact of being officially forced to leave an organisation _____
6. basic, and not detailed or developed _____
7. moral or legal entitlements to have or do something _____
8. a situation that could possibly happen _____
9. negative comments, judgements _____
10. an animal before it is born, beginning to develop _____
11. coordinated a situation to produce a desired effect, especially in a secret way _____
12. extremely violent and cruel _____
13. the fair administration of laws so that all people, regardless of ethnic origin, gender, etc are treated without prejudice _____
14. provided with money for a particular purpose _____
15. inserted or fixed into a body, especially by surgery _____
16. feeling extremely angry without showing it _____

© MR STEGGELS ADVANCED INSTRUCTION PTY LTD

Unit 4

Word usage—complete the sentences using the words in bold from the previous page

1. Civil _____ protect the freedom of individuals in society.

2. The riot was _____ by a minority group of protestors.

3. The country was sanctioned for its _____ treatment of prisoners.

4. The coach finds _____ of his team's performance hard to accept.

5. The Opposition is calling for the _____ of three members of Parliament.

6. A surgically _____ hearing aid can improve or correct hearing loss.

7. Construction on the theme park was _____ when the developer ran out of money to pay contractors.

8. I will use a _____ for my novel as I am a very private person.

9. The College of Advanced Robotics is _____ by a private company.

10. After years of smoking, his teeth were a _____ yellow colour.

11. _____ is based on the idea that all people are equal.

12. When I walked out of the subway, I had to pause to get my _____.

13. The man was _____ when he realised that his new car had been stolen.

14. The most likely _____ is that the manager will resign after the company posts huge losses this financial year.

15. Even though children's artwork tends to be _____, many people think it is an important means of self-expression.

16. After the eighth week of development, a human _____ is called a foetus.

Unit 5

Definitions—match the words in the bold with their meanings below

professional	**lingering**	**pristine**	**transplant**
testimonial	**buffed**	**initiated**	**dreaded**
rumba	**acquaintance**	**macramé**	**donor**
practically	**slurry**	**flailing**	**retrovirus**

1. caused something to begin   _____
2. a person that you have met but do not know well   _____
3. belonging to a paid profession in which one is educated and highly skilled; a person skilled in a particular activity   _____
4. new, in very good condition; untouched natural environment   _____
5. a medical operation in which a new organ is put into someone's body   _____
6. rubbed an object made of metal, wood, or leather using a soft, dry cloth in order to make it shine   _____
7. a person who gives some of their blood or a part of their body to help someone who is ill   _____
8. a statement about the character or qualities of someone or something   _____
9. a mixture of water and small pieces of a solid; another word for scrawled mess   _____
10. taking a long time to leave or disappear   _____
11. almost or very nearly   _____
12. regarded or anticipated with fear or worry   _____
13. the art of joining pieces of string together in knots to form a decorative pattern; the items produced using this art form   _____
14. family of enveloped viruses that replicate in a host cell through the process of reverse transcription   _____
15. moving energetically in an uncontrolled way   _____
16. a type of dancing, originally from Cuba, or such music   _____

© MR STEGGELS ADVANCED INSTRUCTION PTY LTD

Unit 5

Word usage—complete the sentences using the words in bold from the previous page

1. The groom _____ his dress shoes in preparation for the wedding ceremony.

2. It is _____ impossible for me to get home in less than an hour in this traffic.

3. HIV is an example of a _____; a disease that destroys the body's ability to fight infection.

4. The competitors had to perform the _____ in the third round of the dance championship.

5. 'Are you a regular blood _____?' asked the nurse, before taking my blood.

6. He has only been playing football as a _____ for two years.

7. After his heart _____, the man had a new lease on life.

8. The fashion designer's website featured a _____ from a famous model.

9. I am selling my Ferrari; it is only two months old and is in _____ condition.

10. I could not keep up with the pace of the lecture and so my book was a _____ of scribbled notes.

11. I made an important new business _____ at the conference this year.

12. After the performance had finished, fans were _____ at the stage door, hoping to catch sight of the lead actor.

13. A wasp flew towards me and I began _____ my arms about in terror.

14. I had worked hard to make a _____ wall hanging for Mother's Day.

15. 'Who _____ the food fight in the cafeteria?' the principal demanded.

16. In the coming holiday break, my _____ cousin, who is a terrible bully, is coming to stay with us.

© MR STEGGELS ADVANCED INSTRUCTION PTY LTD

Unit 6

Definitions—match the words in the bold with their meanings below

scholastic	stray	drat	honors
finance	penal	inwardly	senator
feat	beastly	publicity	discrimination
persevere	exhilarated	career	sack

1. of or relating to punishment given by law _____
2. very unkind or unpleasant _____
3. relating to school and education _____
4. to travel along a route that was not originally intended; deviate or wander off _____
5. the series of jobs that you do during your working life _____
6. the money needed to make something happen _____
7. the activity of making certain that someone or something attracts a lot of interest or attention from many people _____
8. a politician who has been elected to a Senate _____
9. an achievement needing a lot of skill, strength, courage _____
10. to remove someone from their job _____
11. treating a person or particular group of people differently, especially in a worse way because of skin, colour, gender etc _____
12. used when you are slightly annoyed _____
13. a public reward, prize, or title that expresses appreciation for unusual achievement _____
14. very excited and happy _____
15. in a way that is inside your mind and not expressed openly _____
16. to try to do or continue doing something in a determined way despite having problems _____

Unit 6

Word usage—complete the sentences using the words in bold from the previous page

1. The local council has refused to _____ the new skate park because it will encourage anti-social behaviour.

2. Two workers got the _____ for fighting in the warehouse.

3. Any form of _____ in the workplace will not be tolerated.

4. The scientist will _____ with his plan to cure the common cold, even though no one has come close to finding a cure before.

5. Only one _____ voted against the bill to make bicycle helmets compulsory.

6. The school medal is awarded for outstanding _____ achievement.

7. If the fence is not closed, the herd of cattle is able to _____ onto the road.

8. The Eiffel Tower is a remarkable _____ of engineering.

9. I was _____ relieved that the exam had been postponed for a week.

10. He's hoping for a _____ as a forensic scientist with the police force.

11. 'Wesley, why are you being so _____ to your sister?' demanded Mother. 'Stop pulling her hair!'

12. 'Oh _____!' cried the witch. 'I've run out of poisoned apples again.'

13. The suspect had been in and out of _____ institutions from the age of sixteen.

14. The valiant soldier was buried with full military _____.

15. At the end of the marathon race, I was _____ as I had come first!

16. The intense _____ surrounding the case will make a fair trial impossible.

© MR STEGGELS ADVANCED INSTRUCTION PTY LTD

Unit 7

Definitions—match the words in the bold with their meanings below

incensed	pungent	souvenir	allege
pacify	awestruck	wrenched	pact
bade	odour	in-house	contributions
decreed	marveled	rounded	cyclical

1. showed or experienced great surprise _____

2. a smell, often one that is unpleasant _____

3. happening in cycles; recurrent _____

4. officially decided or ordered that something must happen _____

5. uttered a greeting or farewell; commanded or ordered to do something _____

6. filled with feelings of admiration or respect _____

7. extremely angry; enraged _____

8. to say that something is true or that someone has done something wrong, although it has not been proved _____

9. to cause someone who is angry or upset to be calm and satisfied _____

10. went around something such as a bend or the corner of a building; moved on in a new direction _____

11. a formal agreement between two groups, countries, or people, especially to help each other or to stop fighting _____

12. done by employees within an organisation rather than by other companies or independent workers _____

13. something you buy or keep to help you remember a holiday or special event _____

14. very strong, sometimes unpleasantly strong _____

15. things you give or do in order to help something be successful _____

16. twisted and pulled something roughly from the place where it was being held _____

Unit 7

Word usage—complete the sentences using the words in bold from the previous page

1. The tourists _____ at the sight of Niagara Falls.

2. I _____ my friends good night and retired to my bedroom.

3. The prosecution will _____ that the police officer accepted bribes.

4. Many companies contract out jobs that they are unable to do _____.

5. After the concert was cut short, police were called in to _____ the crowd.

6. At the zoo, I was overcome by the _____ smell of the goat exhibit.

7. The locker room was filled with the unmistakable _____ of sweaty feet.

8. Following the war, the two countries signed a non-aggression _____.

9. He bought a model of a red bus as a _____ of his trip to London.

10. The residents were _____ at the decision to close their local school.

11. After the earthquake, the government _____ that all new buildings must be built according to strict standards.

12. From the _____ expression on the buyer's face, I could tell that he was impressed with the beachfront property.

13. As they _____ the bend and came in sight of the river, Philip took his girlfriend's hand and asked her to marry him.

14. Economists must try to predict _____ changes in the economy.

15. All _____ to charities are tax deductible.

16. The assailant _____ the handbag from the woman's hands.

© MR STEGGELS ADVANCED INSTRUCTION PTY LTD

Unit 8

Definitions—match the words in the bold with their meanings below

immaculate	preceded	questionable	vegetation
subdued	dismissed	fictionalised	hoax
lethargic	freelance	serial	salinity
queasy	income	fad	aquifer

1. doing work for different organisations rather than working all the time for a single company _____
2. plants in general, or plants that are found in a particular area _____
3. removed someone from their job, especially because they have done something wrong _____
4. perfectly clean or tidy _____
5. a style or interest that is very popular for a short period of time _____
6. went before something or someone in time or space _____
7. not certain, or wrong in some way _____
8. not as happy as usual or quieter than usual _____
9. containing or consisting of salt; a measure of the level of salt _____
10. wrote about a real event or character with added imaginary details and altered facts _____
11. a layer of rock, sand, or earth that contains water or allows water to pass through it _____
12. money that is earned from doing work or received from investments _____
13. likely to vomit _____
14. having little energy; feeling unwilling and unable to do anything _____
15. a story on television or radio or in a newspaper, that is broadcast or printed in separate parts _____
16. a humorous or malicious deception; to trick or deceive _____

Unit 8

Word usage—complete the sentences using the words in bold from the previous page

1. Some people believe that the moon landing in 1969 was an elaborate _____.

2. The groom was dressed in an _____ white suit.

3. The farmer discovered a natural _____ on his property.

4. _____ is a problem for many famers as it impacts on crop production.

5. The flu had left me feeling very _____ so I remained indoors all week.

6. After failing to make the final, the champion swimmer was _____.

7. A science experiment is often _____ by a summary of results.

8. After the fourth ride on the Whirly Bird spinning coaster, I was feeling _____.

9. The railway track will have to be cleared of _____ if it is to be used again for transporting freight.

10. Wearing ripped jeans is the latest _____ among teenagers.

11. The life of the famous inventor had been _____ in order to make a dramatic film that would attract a wide audience.

12. Many journalists work _____ for several publications.

13. Her romance novel is being turned into a TV _____ .

14. The manager was _____ from his job for incompetence.

15. Most late-night television is of _____ value.

16. I haven't had much _____ from my stocks and shares this year.

Unit 9

Definitions—match the words in the bold with their meanings below

contemplating	**industrial**	**hoisted**	**desalination**
consequences	**theory**	**focused**	**resources**
skewered	**fate**	**implements**	**resistant**
bleating	**sighted**	**musty**	**possess**

1. in or related to factories; designed for use in industry　_____

2. managed to see or observe; caught an initial glimpse of　_____

3. the results of a particular action or situation, often bad or inconvenient　_____

4. lifted something heavy, sometimes using ropes or a machine　_____

5. the typical sound made by sheep or goats; complaining　_____

6. put pieces of food, especially meat, on a rod of thin metal　_____

7. the process of removing salt from sea water　_____

8. considering a possible future action, or considering one particular thing for a long time in a serious and quiet way　_____

9. useful or valuable possessions or quality of a country, organisation, or person　_____

10. a formal statement of the rules on which a subject of study is based or of ideas that are suggested to explain a fact or event　_____

11. to have or own something, or to have a particular quality　_____

12. a power that some people believe causes and controls all events; that we cannot change or control the future　_____

13. not wanting to accept something, especially changes or new ideas; unable to be penetrated　_____

14. giving a lot of attention to one particular thing　_____

15. smelling unpleasantly old and slightly wet　_____

16. tools that work by being moved by hand　_____

Unit 9

Word usage—complete the sentences using the words in bold from the previous page

1. We recently purchased stain-_____ carpet for our hallways.

2. Our teacher is always _____ about our poor grammar.

3. At age fifty, the man was _____ a change of career.

4. The government spent one billion dollars to build a _____ plant, fearing that fresh water may run out.

5. If you break the law, you must face the _____ of your actions.

6. Japan underwent significant _____ expansion after World War II.

7. The geologist has a _____ that the crater was caused by a meteorite.

8. I cut up the meat into chunks and _____ them to make kebabs.

9. The library basement was full of _____ old books.

10. With some difficulty, he _____ the injured ewe onto his shoulders.

11. There is a need for more _____ research in the area of flu vaccine.

12. When we met again by chance, I felt it must be _____ that we were meant to be together.

13. The abandoned ship was _____ off the coast of New Guinea.

14. Shopkeepers are not supposed to sell knives and other sharp _____ to children.

15. In the past, the root of this plant was thought to _____ magical powers.

16. Britain's mineral _____ include coal and gas deposits.

Unit 10

Definitions—match the words in the bold with their meanings below

panacea	**regrettable**	**luminescent**	**incredulous**
besmirched	**eisteddfod**	**odyssey**	**cavalcade**
succumb	**naturopathy**	**physician**	**elucidate**
biodegradable	**differentiate**	**vigilance**	**contemptible**

1. something that will solve all problems _____

2. giving rise to feelings of sadness, repentance or disappointment _____

3. producing a soft light _____

4. not wanting or able to believe something, and showing this _____

5. said things about someone to negatively influence other people's opinion of them _____

6. an organised series of acts and performances usually in one place; a drama festival _____

7. a long, exciting journey _____

8. a line of people, vehicles, horses, etc. following a particular route as part of a ceremony; a formal procession _____

9. to lose the determination to oppose; to accept defeat _____

10. a system of treating diseases using natural methods such as controlling what a person eats, exercise; homeopathy _____

11. a medical doctor who has general skill; not a surgeon _____

12. to explain something or make something clear _____

13. identify differences, make something appear or become different in the process of growth or development _____

14. the state of keeping careful watch for possible danger _____

15. deserving hatred because a person or thing is worthless or beneath consideration _____

16. capable of being decomposed or broken down by bacteria or other living organisms; non-polluting _____

Unit 10

Word usage—complete the sentences using the words in bold from the previous page

1. Despite its popularity, technology is not a _____ for all our problems.

2. His reputation had been _____ by malicious gossip on social media.

3. The _____ proceeded through the city along streets lined with well-wishers.

4. _____ packaging helps to limit the amount of harmful chemicals released into the atmosphere.

5. Police said that it was due to the _____ of a neighbour that the fire was discovered before it could spread.

6. The teacher has to _____ each lesson to cater for the various levels of ability among students.

7. If you don't clean the wound, you may _____ to an infection.

8. I was nervous about performing a solo violin piece at the _____.

9. Her decision to leave the cast at such a late stage in rehearsals was _____.

10. My doctor offers alternative therapies and has a qualification in _____.

11. The judge described the violent robbery of the elderly man as _____.

12. You will have to _____ your position more clearly; I cannot understand your argument for banning school students on public transport.

13. The actress gave an _____ stare when her rival won the award for best performance in a film.

14. The family _____ made a house call to treat the ill children.

15. The movie is about a boy's _____ to find his parents after he is separated from them during the Korean War.

16. Shrouded in fog, the moon cast a _____ glow on the surface of the lake.

© MR STEGGELS ADVANCED INSTRUCTION PTY LTD

Test 1

1. Which word means **a quality of grace in the way a person holds or moves their body**?

    A   pitch
    B   poise
    C   pacify
    D   professional

2. Choose the best meaning of the word **persevere**

    A   in a way that shows a feeling of wanting something or someone very much
    B   careful thoughts about a particular subject or issue before making a decision
    C   taking a long time to leave or disappear
    D   to continue doing something in a determined way despite having problems

3. Choose the word that is closest in meaning to **stray**

    A   drift
    B   wander
    C   deviate
    D   all of the above

4. Choose the word that is most opposite in meaning to **pacify**

    A   anger
    B   admire
    C   calm
    D   deceive

5. Which is a royal ceremony?

    A   eisteddfod
    B   coronation
    C   testimonial
    D   cavalcade

6. Choose the words that best complete the sentence

    We were _____ when we first _____ the Grand Canyon.

    A   focused   fictionalised
    B   awestruck   sighted
    C   pacified   decreed
    D   incredulous   rounded

7. The letters in **eielltbt** can be rearranged to make a word meaning

    A   moral or legal entitlements to have or do something
    B   extremely violent and cruel
    C   to happen after something else, especially as a result of it
    D   to make a person or an action seem as if he, she or it is not important

8. Which pair of words is closest in meaning?

    A   pacify   pact
    B   beastly   barbarous
    C   regrettable   questionable
    D   lingering   longingly

9. Which word is most opposite in meaning to **putrid**?

    A   immaculate
    B   besmirched
    C   musty
    D   queasy

10. Which word should replace the words in bold in the following sentence?

    I smiled but **in a way that was inside my mind and not expressed openly**, I was very angry.

    A   longingly
    B   inwardly
    C   flailing
    D   practically

11. Choose the words that best complete the sentence

    The pirates who _____ the village were captured and sent to a _____ colony.

A	buffed	scholastic
B	besmirched	social justice
C	wrenched	forensic
D	plundered	penal

12. Choose the word that is most similar in meaning to **genetically-modified**

    A implanted
    B engineered
    C transplanted
    D orchestrated

13. Someone who is **incredulous** can best be described as

    A disbelieving
    B unconvinced
    C doubtful
    D all of the above

14. A problem for farmers is increasing levels of

    A desalination
    B salinity
    C retrovirus
    D panacea

15. Choose the words that best complete the following sentence

    The government is _____ building a _____ plant to provide fresh drinking water during extended periods of drought.

A	contemplating	desalination
B	focused on	genetically-modified
C	instinctively	aquifer
D	practically	biodegradable

© MR STEGGELS ADVANCED INSTRUCTION PTY LTD

16. Choose the words that best complete the sentence

    Hoping to pursue a _____ in _____, I enrolled at university to study Economics.

    A   theory   naturopathy
    B   fad   social justice
    C   career   finance
    D   profession   physician

17. Which is a **disease**?

    A   cholesterol
    B   retrovirus
    C   salinity
    D   diabetes

18. Which pair of words is closest in meaning?

    A   precede   decreed
    B   pungent   luminescent
    C   subdued   forlorn
    D   lingering   musty

19. Choose the best definition of the word **vigilance**

    A   the state of keeping careful watch for possible danger
    B   expressing negative comments or judgments
    C   careful and controlled
    D   mental or emotional strain

20. Which word should replace the words in bold in the following sentence?

    I stared at the slice of chocolate cake **in a way that showed a feeling of wanting it very much**.

    A   practically
    B   lingeringly
    C   longingly
    D   instinctively

© MR STEGGELS ADVANCED INSTRUCTION PTY LTD

Test 2

1. Which word means **a large amount of money that is demanded in exchange for someone who has been taken prisoner**?

    A   finance
    B   income
    C   ransom
    D   hoax

2. Choose the best meaning of the word **endowment**

    A   a ceremony at which a person is made king or queen
    B   money that is given to a college, hospital, etc. in order to provide it with an income
    C   money earned from working
    D   a public reward, prize, or title that expresses appreciation for unusual achievement

3. Choose the word that is closest in meaning to **elucidate**

    A   explain
    B   discuss
    C   argue
    D   entertain

4. Choose the word that is most opposite in meaning to **ensue**

    A   decree
    B   possess
    C   hoist
    D   precede

5. Which is an item of clothing?

    A   leotard
    B   fad
    C   macramé
    D   rumba

© MR STEGGELS ADVANCED INSTRUCTION PTY LTD

6. Choose the word that best completes the sentence

   Popular music appeals to _____ audiences.

   A   mainstream
   B   incredulous
   C   awestruck
   D   obsessed

7. The letters in **botoa** can be rearranged to make a word meaning

   A   a situation that could possibly happen
   B   sense of place
   C   an action or word that is avoided for religious or social reasons
   D   to direct onto a target

8. Choose the word that is closest in meaning to **succumb**

   A   surrender
   B   resist
   C   pacify
   D   linger

9. Which pair of words is most opposite in meaning?

   A   marveled   sighted
   B   rudimentary   industrial
   C   flailing   succumb
   D   social justice   discrimination

10. Which word should replace the words in bold in the following sentence?

    In 1986, she was made a saint for her **strong belief in a religion shown in the way she lived.**

    A   piety
    B   social justice
    C   vigilance
    D   contributions

© MR STEGGELS ADVANCED INSTRUCTION PTY LTD

11. Choose the best word to complete the sentence

   I decided to keep as a _____ one of the _____ I had dug up from the gold fields.

A	souvenir	implements
B	fad	resources
C	endowment	bearings
D	panacea	rights

12. Which word means the same as **lifted**?

   A   skewered
   B   wrenched
   C   hoisted
   D   implanted

13. Items that are **biodegradable** are also

   A   orchestrated
   B   cyclical
   C   resources
   D   non-polluting

14. Choose the word that is most closely related to **scholastic**

   A   law
   B   education
   C   politics
   D   medicine

15. Choose the best meaning for **regrettable**

   A   not certain, wrong in some way
   B   deserving hatred because a person or thing is worthless or beneath consideration
   C   giving rise to feelings of sadness, repentance or disappointment
   D   not as happy as usual or quieter than usual

© MR STEGGELS ADVANCED INSTRUCTION PTY LTD

16. Choose the words that best complete the sentence

   She was awarded _____ for her performance at the ballet _____.

   A   income   odyssey
   B   piety   coronation
   C   uniformly   feat
   D   honours   eisteddfod

17. Choose the best meaning for **fad**

   A   something difficult needing a lot of skill, strength, courage
   B   used when you are slightly annoyed
   C   a humorous or malicious deception; to trick or deceive
   D   a style or interest that is very popular for a short period of time

18. Choose the word that refers to **the distance between two waves of energy**

   A   spectrometer
   B   wavelength
   C   cavalcade
   D   monochromatic

19. The letters in **caciclyl** can be rearranged to make a word meaning

   A   recurrent
   B   unpleasant
   C   twisted
   D   remove

20. Which word should replace the words in bold in the following sentence?

   The room was **smelling unpleasantly old and slightly wet** so I opened a window.

   A   lingering
   B   putrid
   C   musty
   D   odour

© MR STEGGELS ADVANCED INSTRUCTION PTY LTD

Test 3

1. Which word means **an improvement to something that makes it worth more**?

    A differentiated
    B unadulterated
    C value-added
    D engineered

2. Choose the best meaning of the word **in lieu**

    A to happen after something else
    B to come before something or someone in time or space
    C instead of
    D provided with money for a particular purpose

3. Choose the word that is closest in meaning to **godlike**?

    A awestruck
    B luminescent
    C formidable
    D sacred

4. Choose the word that is most opposite in meaning to **colourful**

    A monochromatic
    B flailing
    C dreaded
    D rudimentary

5. Which is a style of music?

    A rumba
    B in-house
    C Victorian
    D taboo

6. Choose the word that best completes the sentence

   Fortunately, the dog had a microchip _____ in its neck so we were able to locate the owner easily.

   A   wrenched
   B   imposed
   C   implanted
   D   donor

7. The letters in **receded** can be rearranged to make a word meaning

   A   uttered a greeting or farewell; commanded or ordered to do something
   B   officially decided or ordered that something must happen
   C   said things about someone to negatively influence other people's opinion of them
   D   producing a soft light

8. Which word should replace the words in bold in the following sentence?

   They spend most of their **money that is earned from doing work** on rent and food.

   A   finance
   B   endowment
   C   contributions
   D   income

9. Choose the best word to complete the sentence

   As the ball came flying toward my head, I _____ put my hand up to catch it.

   A   uniformly
   B   inwardly
   C   instinctively
   D   practically

10. What is another word for a formal procession?

    A   coronation
    B   panacea
    C   cavalcade
    D   odyssey

© MR STEGGELS ADVANCED INSTRUCTION PTY LTD

11. Choose the best word to complete the sentence

    The valuable items were stolen due to a serious _____ in security.

    A   bleating
    B   vigilance
    C   breach
    D   feat

12. The letters in **underdo** can be rearranged to make a word meaning

    A   happening in cycles
    B   twisted and pulled something roughly from the place where it was being held
    C   went around something such as a bend or corner
    D   uttered a greeting or farewell

13. Which is most likely to be **auctioned**?

    A   property
    B   bids
    C   finance
    D   contributions

14. What is the best definition of **funded**?

    A   doing work for different organisations rather than working for a single company
    B   money that is earned from doing work or received from investments
    C   the money needed to make something happen
    D   provided with money for a particular purpose

15. Which is a type of **evidence**?

    A   monochromatic
    B   forensic
    C   biodegradable
    D   serial

© MR STEGGELS ADVANCED INSTRUCTION PTY LTD

16. Choose the word that best completes the sentence

    A diet with too many animal products may lead to high levels of_____.

    A   diabetes
    B   lethargy
    C   cholesterol
    D   vegetation

17. The letters in **myrobe** can be rearranged to make a word meaning

    A   pure
    B   an animal before it is born, beginning to develop and grow
    C   basic, and not detailed or developed
    D   moral or legal entitlements to have or do something

18. Whose word is most closely associated with **donor**?

    A   naturopathy
    B   transplant
    C   implant
    D   micron

19. Another word for **unadulterated** is

    A   taboo
    B   pure
    C   beastly
    D   immaculate

20. Which word should replace the words in bold in the following sentence?

    Some people are unable to **identify differences** between fact and opinion.

    A   succumb
    B   elucidate
    C   home in
    D   differentiate

© MR STEGGELS ADVANCED INSTRUCTION PTY LTD

Test 4

1. Which word means **producing a soft light**?

    A   luminescent
    B   pungent
    C   lingering
    D   mainstream

2. Choose the best meaning of the word **theory**

    A   the results of a particular action or situation
    B   a story on television or radio or in a newspaper in separate parts
    C   a formal agreement between two groups
    D   an idea that is suggested to explain a fact or event

3. Which word is most opposite in meaning to **exhilarated**?

    A   queasy
    B   forlorn
    C   rejected
    D   incensed

4. Which is most similar in meaning to **sack**?

    A   dismiss
    B   besmirch
    C   belittle
    D   stray

5. Which is used to help sell a product or service?

    A   serial
    B   physician
    C   a testimonial
    D   Senator

© MR STEGGELS ADVANCED INSTRUCTION PTY LTD

6. Choose the words that best complete the sentence

   _____ was directed at the _____ for failing to diagnose the patient's condition sooner.

   A   Evidence   missionaries
   B   Publicity   Senator
   C   Vigilance   professional
   D   Criticism   physician

7. The letters in **geleal** can be rearranged to make a word meaning

   A   officially decided or ordered that something must happen
   B   to say that someone has done something wrong, although it has not been proved
   C   making certain that someone or something attracts a lot of interest
   D   moving energetically in an uncontrolled way

8. Which word should replace the words in bold in the following sentence?

   The **most important part** of his argument is that prisons do not rehabilitate people.

   A   endowment
   B   theory
   C   criticism
   D   essence

9. Which of the following can be **buffed**?

   A   leather
   B   metal
   C   wood
   D   all of the above

10. Which words should replace the words in bold in the following sentence?

    I am **giving a lot of attention to** my studies this year.

    A   obsessed by
    B   resistant to
    C   focused on
    D   lethargic about

11. Choose the words that best complete the following sentence

    Crop circles attract great _____ but are nothing more than a _____.

A	criticism	panacea
B	publicity	hoax
C	income	souvenir
D	honours	ransom

12. Which word is most similar in meaning to **obsessed**?

    A   possessed
    B   focused
    C   incredulous
    D   awestruck

13. An author who wishes to remain **anonymous** may use

    A   a pseudonym
    B   a hoax
    C   a cipher
    D   publicity

14. Which word should replace the words in bold in the following sentence?

    Her failure to get an interview for the position will **severely damage** her self-confidence.

    A   shatter
    B   slurry
    C   skewer
    D   elucidate

15. Which word is most opposite to **halted**?

    A   initiated
    B   preceded
    C   bade
    D   breached

© MR STEGGELS ADVANCED INSTRUCTION PTY LTD

16. Choose the words that best complete the sentence

    The stomach virus made me feel _____ and _____.

    A   beastly   exhilarated
    B   seething   besmirched
    C   queasy   lethargic
    D   putrid   pungent

17. The letters in **deafinrr** can be rearranged to make a word meaning

    A   to direct onto a target
    B   producing a soft light
    C   a type of light that feels warm but cannot be seen
    D   the distance between two waves of energy, or the length of the radio wave

18. Which is presented in a court of law as proof of innocence or guilt?

    A   theory
    B   evidence
    C   resources
    D   surveillance

19. Choose the best meaning of the word **odyssey**

    A   family of enveloped viruses that replicate in a host cell
    B   something done in a determined way, despite having problems
    C   a story on television or radio or in a newspaper in separate parts
    D   a long, exciting journey

20. Choose the word that best completes the sentence

    There are many _____ to take into account before we move interstate.

    A   consequences
    B   contributions
    C   considerations
    D   implements

© MR STEGGELS ADVANCED INSTRUCTION PTY LTD

Test 5

1. Which word means **the careful watching of a person or place due to possible criminal activity**?

    A   social justice
    B   surveillance
    C   testimony
    D   sighting

2. Choose the best meaning of the word **expulsion**

    A   the fact of being officially forced to leave an organisation or activity
    B   to remove someone from their job
    C   of or relating to punishment given by law
    D   commanded or ordered to do something

3. Another word for **uniformly** is

    A   consistently
    B   evenly
    C   unchangingly
    D   all of the above

4. Something that is **rudimentary** is not

    A   polite
    B   highly developed
    C   in very good condition
    D   regarded with fear or worry

5. Which is used to encode a secret message?

    A   spectrometer
    B   pseudonym
    C   scenario
    D   cipher

© MR STEGGELS ADVANCED INSTRUCTION PTY LTD

6. Choose the words that best complete the sentence

    The _____ was forced to reveal his political _____.

    A   senator   contributions
    B   physician   consequences
    C   professional   finance
    D   acquaintance   income

7. The letters in **coarseni** can be rearranged to make a word meaning

    A   a situation that could possibly happen
    B   a mixture of water and small pieces of a solid
    C   moving energetically in an uncontrolled way
    D   a public reward, prize, or title that expresses appreciation for unusual achievement

8. Which word should replace the words in bold in the following sentence?

    The council says that it doesn't have enough **useful or valuable possessions** to deal with graffiti.

    A   contributions
    B   consequences
    C   resources
    D   bearings

9. Choose the best words to complete the sentence

    Water that has been filtered through the _____ is _____.

    A   panacea   sacred
    B   mainstream   putrid
    C   aquifer   pristine
    D   spectrometer   pungent

10. Which is black in colour?

    A   pitch
    B   slurry
    C   embryo
    D   cholesterol

11. Which word is both a verb (action) and a noun (a thing)?

    A   hedge
    B   allege
    C   bade
    D   buffed

12. Choose the word most opposite in meaning to **dismissed**

    A   sighted
    B   expelled
    C   preceded
    D   retained

13. Which word should replace the words in bold in the following sentence?

    He had **said things about me to negatively influence other people's opinion of** my reputation.

    A   dismissed
    B   besmirched
    C   plundered
    D   skewered

14. Choose the word most similar in meaning to **incensed**

    A   exhilarated
    B   subdued
    C   seething
    D   none of the above

15. Something that is **designed for use in a factory** is

    A   industrial
    B   engineered
    C   orchestrated
    D   genetically-modified

© MR STEGGELS ADVANCED INSTRUCTION PTY LTD

16. Choose the word that best completes the sentence

    Recent high unemployment figures show that the _____ is not performing well.

    A   economy
    B   finance
    C   income
    D   funding

17. The letters in **readded** can be rearranged to make a word meaning

    A   having overwhelming strength, size or power
    B   uttered a greeting or farewell
    C   ordered that something must happen
    D   regarded or anticipated with fear or worry

18. What might be made and given as a gift?

    A   piety
    B   hedge
    C   serial
    D   macramé

19. Which words best complete the following sentence?

    Upon entering the kitchen, I detected the _____ _____ of boiled cabbage.

    A   forensic   evidence
    B   questionable   essence
    C   pungent   odour
    D   musty   vegetation

20. Choose the category to which the other three belong

    A   senator
    B   career
    C   naturopath
    D   physician

Solutions

Unit 1

Definitions

1	poise	5	auction	9	longingly	13	retained
2	imposing	6	Victorian	10	cholesterol	14	forlorn
3	leotard	7	forensic	11	diabetes	15	hedge
4	instinctively	8	value-added	12	engineered	16	genetically-modified

Word usage

1	value-added	5	retained	9	diabetes	13	Victorian
2	cholesterol	6	imposing	10	forensic	14	genetically-modified
3	auction	7	hedge	11	instinctively	15	forlorn
4	engineered	8	longingly	12	poise	16	leotard

Unit 2

Definitions

1	cipher	5	pitch	9	essence	13	missionaries
2	considerations	6	obsessed	10	god-like	14	spectrometer
3	economy	7	shatter	11	sacred	15	infrared
4	ransom	8	uniformly	12	surveillance	16	evidence

Word usage

1	infrared	5	surveillance	9	considerations	13	obsessed
2	spectrometer	6	shatter	10	sacred	14	missionaries
3	ransom	7	economy	11	uniformly	15	godlike
4	evidence	8	pitch	12	essence	16	cipher

Unit 3

Definitions

1	belittle	5	formidable	9	plundered	13	wavelength
2	ensue	6	in lieu	10	monochromatic	14	mainstream
3	coronation	7	breach	11	taboo	15	home in
4	endowment	8	piety	12	unadulterated	16	micron

© MR STEGGELS ADVANCED INSTRUCTION PTY LTD

Unit 3

Word usage

1	plundered	5	in lieu	9	ensue	13	micron
2	coronation	6	breach	10	belittle	14	home in
3	endowment	7	formidable	11	unadulterated	15	mainstream
4	taboo	8	monochromatic	12	piety	16	wavelength

Unit 4

Definitions

1	putrid	5	expulsion	9	criticism	13	social justice
2	bearings	6	rudimentary	10	embryo	14	funded
3	pseudonym	7	rights	11	orchestrated	15	implanted
4	halted	8	scenario	12	barbarous	16	seething

Word usage

1	rights	5	expulsion	9	funded	13	seething
2	orchestrated	6	implanted	10	putrid	14	scenario
3	barbarous	7	halted	11	social justice	15	rudimentary
4	criticism	8	pseudonym	12	bearings	16	embryo

Unit 5

Definitions

1	initiated	5	transplant	9	slurry	13	macramé
2	acquaintance	6	buffed	10	lingering	14	retrovirus
3	professional	7	donor	11	practically	15	flailing
4	pristine	8	testimonial	12	dreaded	16	rumba

Word usage

1	buffed	5	donor	9	pristine	13	flailing
2	practically	6	professional	10	slurry	14	macramé
3	retrovirus	7	transplant	11	acquaintance	15	initiated
4	rumba	8	testimonial	12	lingering	16	dreaded

© MR STEGGELS ADVANCED INSTRUCTION PTY LTD

Unit 6

Definitions

1	penal	5	career	9	feat	13	honours
2	beastly	6	finance	10	sack	14	exhilarated
3	scholastic	7	publicity	11	discrimination	15	inwardly
4	stray	8	senator	12	drat	16	persevere

Word usage

1	finance	5	senator	9	inwardly	13	penal
2	sack	6	scholastic	10	career	14	honours
3	discrimination	7	stray	11	beastly	15	exhilarated
4	persevere	8	feat	12	drat	16	publicity

Unit 7

Definitions

1	awestruck	5	bade	9	pacify	13	souvenir
2	odour	6	marveled	10	rounded	14	pungent
3	cyclical	7	incensed	11	pact	15	contributions
4	decreed	8	allege	12	in-house	16	wrenched

Word usage

1	marveled	5	pacify	9	souvenir	13	rounded
2	bade	6	pungent	10	incensed	14	cyclical
3	allege	7	odour	11	decreed	15	contributions
4	in-house	8	pact	12	awestruck	16	wrenched

Unit 8

Definitions

1	freelance	5	fad	9	salinity	13	queasy
2	vegetation	6	preceded	10	fictionalised	14	lethargic
3	dismissed	7	questionable	11	aquifer	15	serial
4	immaculate	8	subdued	12	income	16	hoax

© MR STEGGELS ADVANCED INSTRUCTION PTY LTD

Unit 8

Word usage

1	hoax	5	lethargic	9	vegetation	13	serial
2	immaculate	6	subdued	10	fad	14	dismissed
3	aquifer	7	preceded	11	fictionalised	15	questionable
4	salinity	8	queasy	12	freelance	16	income

Unit 9

Definitions

1	industrial	5	bleating	9	resources	13	resistant
2	sighted	6	skewered	10	theory	14	focused
3	consequences	7	desalination	11	possess	15	musty
4	hoisted	8	contemplating	12	fate	16	implements

Word usage

1	resistant	5	consequences	9	musty	13	sighted
2	bleating	6	industrial	10	hoisted	14	implements
3	contemplating	7	theory	11	focused	15	possess
4	desalination	8	skewered	12	fate	16	resources

Unit 10

Definitions

1	panacea	5	besmirched	9	succumb	13	differentiate
2	regrettable	6	eisteddfod	10	naturopathy	14	vigilance
3	luminescent	7	odyssey	11	physician	15	contemptible
4	incredulous	8	cavalcade	12	elucidate	16	biodegradable

Word usage

1	panacea	5	vigilance	9	regrettable	13	incredulous
2	besmirched	6	differentiate	10	naturopathy	14	physician
3	cavalcade	7	succumb	11	contemptible	15	odyssey
4	biodegradable	8	eisteddfod	12	elucidate	16	luminescent

Test 1 solutions

Q	A	Notes
1	B	**poise** refers to a quality of grace in the way a person holds or moves their body
2	D	**persevere** means to continue doing something in a determined way despite having problems
3	D	**stray** means to travel along a route that was not originally intended; **deviate** or **wander** off
4	A	**pacify** means to cause someone who is **angry** or upset to be calm and satisfied
5	B	a **coronation** is a ceremony at which a person is made king or queen
6	B	We were **awestruck** when we first **sighted** the Grand Canyon.
7	D	eielltbt → **belittle** to make a person or an action seem as if he, she or it is not important
8	B	**beastly** very unkind or unpleasant; **barbarous** extremely violent and cruel
9	A	**putrid** means decaying and smelling very bad; **immaculate** means perfectly clean or tidy
10	B	I smiled but **inwardly**, I was very angry.
11	D	The pirates who **plundered** the village were captured and sent to a **penal** colony.
12	B	Something that has been **genetically-modified** has been **engineered**
13	D	**incredulous** means not wanting or able to believe something, and showing this; A, B and C are synonyms of **incredulous**
14	B	**salinity** refers to containing or consisting of salt; a measure of the level of salt
15	A	The government is **contemplating** building a **desalination** plant to provide fresh drinking water during extended periods of drought.
16	C	Hoping to pursue a **career** in **finance**, I enrolled at university to study Economics.
17	D	**diabetes** is a **disease** in which the body cannot control the level of sugar in the blood
18	C	**subdued** means not as happy as usual or quieter than usual; **forlorn** means alone and unhappy
19	A	**vigilance** is the state of keeping careful watch for possible danger
20	C	I stared at the slice of chocolate cake **longingly**.

© MR STEGGELS ADVANCED INSTRUCTION PTY LTD

Test 2 solutions

Q	A	Notes
1	C	a **ransom** is a large amount of money that is demanded in exchange for someone who has been taken prisoner
2	B	an **endowment** is money that is given to a college, hospital, etc. in order to provide it with an income
3	A	**elucidate** means to **explain** something or make something clear
4	D	**ensue** means to happen after something else; **precede** means to come before something or someone in time or space
5	A	a **leotard** is a tight piece of clothing that covers the body but not the legs, usually worn by dancers
6	A	Popular music appeals to **mainstream** audiences.
7	C	**botoa → taboo** an action or word that is avoided for religious or social reasons
8	A	**succumb** means to lose the determination to oppose; to accept defeat; to surrender
9	D	**social justice** the fair administration of laws that all people, regardless of ethnic origin, gender, class, race, religion are to be treated equally and without prejudice; **discrimination** treating a person or particular group of people differently, especially in a worse way because of skin, colour, gender etc
10	A	She was to be made a saint for her **piety**.
11	A	I decided to keep as a **souvenir** one of the **implements** I had dug up from the gold fields.
12	C	**hoisted** means **lifted** something heavy, sometimes using ropes or a machine
13	D	**biodegradable** means capable of being decomposed or broken down by bacteria or other living organisms; **non-polluting**
14	B	**scholastic** means relating to school and education
15	C	**regrettable** means giving rise to feelings of sadness, repentance or disappointment
16	D	She was awarded **honours** for her performance at the ballet **eisteddfod**.
17	D	a **fad** is a style or interest that is very popular for a short period of time
18	B	**wavelength** refers to the distance between two waves of energy
19	A	**caciclyl → cyclical** happening in cycles; **recurrent**
20	C	The room was **musty** so I opened a window.

© MR STEGGELS ADVANCED INSTRUCTION PTY LTD

Test 3 solutions

Q	A	Notes
1	C	**value-added** means an improvement to something that makes it worth more
2	C	**in lieu** means instead of
3	C	**godlike** means having overwhelming strength, size or power; **formidable** means large and powerful, causing fear and respect
4	A	**monochromatic** means using only black, white, and grey, or only one colour
5	A	**rumba** is a type of dancing, originally from Cuba, or such music
6	C	Fortunately, the dog had a microchip **implanted** into its neck so we were able to locate the owner easily.
7	B	**receded** → **decreed** officially decided or ordered that something must happen
8	D	They spend most of their **income** on rent and food.
9	C	As the ball came flying toward my head, I **instinctively** put my hand up to catch it.
10	C	a **cavalcade** is a line of people, vehicles, horses, etc. following a particular route as part of a ceremony; formal procession
11	C	The valuable items were stolen due to a serious **breach** in security.
12	C	**underdo** → **rounded** went around something such as a bend or corner
13	A	an **auction** is a public sale of goods or **property**, where people make higher and higher bids until the goods are sold
14	D	**funded** means provided with money for a particular purpose
15	B	**forensic** means related to scientific methods of solving crimes, involving examining objects or substances—**evidence**—at a crime scene
16	C	A diet with too many animal products may lead to high levels of **cholesterol**.
17	B	**myrobe** → **embryo** an animal before it is born, beginning to develop and grow
18	B	a **donor** is a person who gives a part of their body to help someone who is ill; a **transplant** is a medical operation in which a new organ is put into someone's body
19	B	**unadulterated** means unspoiled by the addition of other substances → **pure**
20	D	Some people are unable to **differentiate** between fact and opinion.

© MR STEGGELS ADVANCED INSTRUCTION PTY LTD

Test 4 solutions

Q	A	Notes
1	A	**luminescent** means producing a soft light
2	D	a **theory** is an idea that is suggested to explain a fact or event
3	B	**exhilarated** means very excited and happy; **forlorn** means alone and unhappy; left alone and not cared for
4	A	**sack** means to remove someone from their job; **dismiss** means to remove someone from their job
5	C	a **testimonial** is a statement about the character or qualities of someone or something
6	D	**Criticism** was directed at the **physician** for failing to diagnose the patient's condition sooner.
7	B	**geleal → allege** to say that someone has done something wrong, although it has not been proved
8	D	The **essence** of his argument is that prisons do not rehabilitate people.
9	D	**buffed** means rubbed an object made of **metal**, **wood**, or **leather** using a soft, dry cloth in order to make it shine
10	C	I am **focused on** my studies this year.
11	B	Crop circles attract great **publicity** but are nothing more than a **hoax**.
12	B	**obsessed** means unable to stop thinking or worrying about something; **focused** means giving a lot of attention to one particular thing
13	A	a **pseudonym** is a name that someone uses that is not their real name, especially for writing a book
14	A	Her failure to get an interview for the position will **shatter** her self-confidence.
15	A	**initiated** means caused something to begin; **halted** means stopped abruptly
16	C	The stomach virus made me feel **queasy** and **lethargic**.
17	C	**deafinrr → infrared** a type of light that feels warm but cannot be seen
18	B	**evidence** means reasons given for believing that something is or is not true
19	D	an **odyssey** is a long, exciting journey
20	C	There are many **considerations** to take into account before we move interstate.

Test 5 solutions

Q	A	Notes
1	B	**surveillance** means the careful watching of a person or place due to possible criminal activity
2	A	**expulsion** means the act of being officially forced to leave an organisation or activity
3	D	**uniformly** means in a way that is the same; not changing or different; evenly
4	B	**rudimentary** means basic, and not detailed or **developed**
5	D	a **cipher** is a system of writing that prevents others from understanding a secret message
6	A	The **senator** was forced to reveal his political **contributions.**
7	A	**coarseni → scenario** a situation that could possibly happen
8	C	The council says that it doesn't have enough **resources** to deal with graffiti.
9	C	Water that has been filtered through the **aquifer** is **pristine**.
10	A	**pitch** is a thick, **black** substance used to waterproof wooden ships; used to describe complete darkness
11	A	**hedge** (verb) to protect or limit something **hedge** (noun) a line of bushes planted very close together along the edge of a garden
12	D	**dismissed** means removed someone from their job; **retained** means kept or continued to have something
13	B	He had **besmirched** my reputation.
14	C	**incensed** means extremely angry; enraged; **seething** means feeling extremely angry without showing it
15	A	**industrial** means in or related to factories; designed for use in industry
16	A	Recent high unemployment figures show that the **economy** is not performing well.
17	D	**readded → dreaded** regarded or anticipated with fear or worry
18	D	**macramé** is the art of joining pieces of string together in knots to form a decorative pattern; the items produced using this art form
19	C	Upon entering the kitchen, I detected the **pungent odour** of boiled cabbage.
20	B	a **career** is the job or series of jobs that you do during your working life. A, C and D are all careers

© MR STEGGELS ADVANCED INSTRUCTION PTY LTD